JN130896

NEWSBREAKS
for **Basic** English Learners
2024

◆ CONTENTS ◆

Donating to Charity
Why is Japan's ranking on the World Giving Index so low?

AP/AFLO

Points for Reading

- ・大谷選手はどのような慈善活動を行いましたか。
- ・海外で慈善活動がさかんな理由は何ですか。

■ 大谷翔平選手

2024 年 3 月には、大谷翔平投手の半生が描かれた絵本『野球しようぜ！大谷翔平ものがたり』が発売されました。大谷選手と出版社は共同で、絵本の売上の一部を日本赤十字社に寄付すると発表しています。

Shohei Ohtani is famous for his charity work.　In 2021 and 2023, he won the Players Choice Award.　The money for this award is given to charity, and the winner can choose the charity.　Ohtani chose a group that helps sick people and their families in California.　After the Noto Earthquake, he and the Los Angeles Dodgers gave $1 million to support the local people. He also gave 60,000 baseball gloves to 20,000 elementary schools in Japan.

05

10

NOTES

00. donate [dóuneit] 寄付する	ロサンゼルス・ドジャース	28. belief [bilíːf] 信念
00. index [índeks] 指数、指標	15. foundation [faundéiʃən]	29. Christian [krístʃən] キリスト教徒
05. winner [wínər] 受賞者	財団、基金	30. Jew [dʒúː] ユダヤ教徒
08. California カリフォルニア州	19. Indonesia インドネシア	30. Muslim [mʌ́zlim] イスラム教徒
08. the Noto Earthquake 能登地震	28. religious [rilídʒəs]	41. the 2011 East Japan Earthquake
09. the Los Angeles Dodgers	宗教的な、宗教の	2011 年東日本大震災

■ ドジャース財団のチャリティーイベントに参加する大谷夫妻
「ブルー・ダイヤモンド・ガラ」と呼ばれるこのイベントは、ロサンゼルスの教育、医療、ホームレス支援などのための資金を集めるためのイベントです。ドジャースの選手やグラミー賞歌手のエド・シーランなどの有名人が出席しました。一般の人々もチケット購入により参加できます。
The Mega Agency/AFLO

RANK	COUNTRY	WORLD GIVING INDEX	HELPED A STRANGER	DONATED MONEY
1	Indonesia	68	61%	82%
2	Ukraine	62	78%	70%
3	Kenya	60	76%	53%
4	United States	58	76%	61%
8	Canada	54	67%	62%
13	Denmark	51	62%	64%
17	United Kingdom	49	51%	71%
137	Afghanistan	20	44%	7%
139	Japan	18	21%	16%

■ World Giving Index rankings 2023（一部抜粋）
World Giving Index（世界寄付指数）は、ここ数か月以内に「助けが必要な見知らぬ人を助けたか？」「ボランティアを行ったか？」などの行動の有無を調査し、その結果を指数化したものです。日本は調査対象の先進国、アジアの国々の中でもともに最下位になっています。
出典：CAF World Giving Index 2023

Giving money to charity is a common thing in most of the world. The Charities Aid Foundation makes a report called the World Giving Index. In this report, it ranks the world's countries for their donations to charity. On the 2023 list, Indonesia was the top country. Over 80% of adults gave money to charity in Indonesia that year. However, Japan is near the bottom of the list. Only 20% of Japanese adults gave to charity, the report says.

Why is Japan's charity ranking so low? The exact reason is unknown, but there are some possible reasons. One is the strong religious beliefs in other countries. For example, Christians, Jews, and Muslims are taught to give money to people in need. For this reason, giving to charity is common in places like Indonesia and the United States. Another reason is that many Japanese people try to solve money problems themselves. One study found that people who think this way are less likely to give to charity.

However, people's feelings toward giving to charity have changed in Japan since the 2011 East Japan Earthquake. That year, about 70% of Japanese people gave money to charities. And in 2020, the amount of money given by Japanese people was 2.5 times the amount 10 years ago. But the amount is still smaller than that of the rest of the world. ■

VOICE DL

The Falling Yen

ドル／円

現在値 (24/ 4/26)

156.08-09
+0.49

The value of a country's money can go up or down

Points for Reading

- ・通貨はどのように売買されていますか。
- ・為替市場の呼び名が変わるのはなぜですか。

■ 156 円台に下落した対ドル円相場（2024 年 4 月 26 日）

2024 年以降、円安のペースが上がっていますが、その要因の 1 つは 2024 年開始の新税制（新 NISA）で、株式投資で得た利益の非課税限度額が大幅に拡大したこととされています。これにより多くの日本人が米国株を購入したことで、ドルの需要が増大しました。その額は毎月 1 兆円程度と言われています。

AFP/AFLO

A huge amount of each country's currency is bought and sold every day. The price for this currency is decided by the seller and the buyer. All buying and selling is done on the internet, so there is no actual currency market in Tokyo or any other city. Daytime in Japan is called the "Tokyo market." 05

NOTES

01. huge [hjúːdʒ] 巨大な
02. currency [kə́ːrənsi] 通貨、貨幣
04. seller [sélər] 売り手
04. buyer [báiər] 買い手
06. actual [ǽktʃuəl] 実在の、現実の
06. market [máːrkit]
　　（金融）市場、マーケット
07. daytime [déitàim] 昼間、昼、日中
08. Tokyo market 東京外国為替市場
09. nighttime [náitàim] 夜間
09. the U.S. 米国
13. New York market
　　ニューヨーク外国為替市場
15. investor [invéstər] 投資家
26. condition [kəndíʃən] 状態
31. crisis [kráisis] 危機、難局
35. as it is now 現在そうであるように
43. change in ～ ～の変化

That is because it is nighttime in the U.S., so much of the buying and selling is done by Japanese people. For the same reason, daytime in New York is called the "New York market."

Most currency is bought and sold through banks by investors, but it is also bought and sold by companies that need foreign currency. Companies need foreign currency for various reasons. For example, Japanese companies with factories in the U.S. need to buy dollars with the yen they get from sales. This is because they need to pay their U.S. workers in dollars.

Why do the buying and selling prices of a country's currency change? One reason is the economic condition of the country. Graph 1 shows the buying and selling prices of the Japanese yen and the

■ 為替仲介取引業者での取引の様子（1987年10月29日）
日本における通貨の売買は、企業や個人、投資家の発注を受けた銀行が、為替仲介取引業者を介して行っています。インターネットが普及する前は主に電話で発注が行われていました。

東洋経済/AFLO

U.S. dollar. From 2007, the value of the dollar fell by nearly 40% over four years. This was because the financial crisis in the U.S. made its economy worse. As a result, a lot of dollars were sold, and the value of the yen rose.

When the value of the yen is low, as it is now, it is not good for companies in Japan that import products from overseas. That is because they need more yen to buy those products than before. On the other hand, companies that export products do not want the yen's value to increase. There are good and bad sides to changes in currency value. However, it is generally believed that a rise in the value of a country's currency is better for its economic future. ■

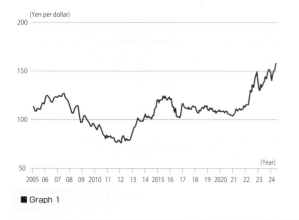

(Yen per dollar)
200

150

100

50

(Year)
2005 06 07 08 09 2010 11 12 13 14 2015 16 17 18 19 2020 21 22 23 24

■ Graph 1

Borderless

■ ウィーン・フィルハーモニー管弦楽団のコンサートで式をする小澤征爾氏（2002 年1月1日）

この日の演奏を収録したCD『ニュー・イヤー・コンサート 2002』は累計売上 80 万枚を記録し、クラシック音楽のCDとしては前例のない大ベスト・セラーを記録しました。

NAGL DIETER/CONTRAST/Gamma/AFLO

Seiji Ozawa was one of the world's best-known conductors

Points for Reading

・小澤征爾氏が指揮者を目指したきっかけとなる出来事はどのようなことでしたか。

Seiji Ozawa was a musician loved by people all over the world. He was famous not only for his musical talent but also for his style and personality. He was able to memorize very difficult pieces of music, and sometimes he conducted without a musical score. When he conducted an orchestra, he moved like he was dancing. And his unique clothing and hairstyle made him stand out.

He first played the piano when he was 10 years old. He wanted to be a pianist, but he broke his fingers

---

NOTES

00. conductor [kəndʌ́ktər] 指揮者
03. talent [tǽlənt] 才能
04. personality [pə̀ːrsənǽləti]
　　個性、人間的魅力
07. musical score 楽譜

28. Yasushi Inoue 井上靖
40. composer [kəmpóuzər] 作曲家
40. Leonard Bernstein
　　レナード・バーンスタイン
43. the New York Philharmonic

ニューヨーク・フィルハーモニック
46. the Boston Symphony Orchestra
　　ボストン交響楽団
49. the Vienna State Opera
　　ウィーン国立歌劇場

■ 長野五輪の開会式での演奏の様子

開会式ではベートーヴェンの「第九 (歓喜の歌)」を演奏しました。第九の終了直後には、ブルーインパルスが聖火台の方向からスモークを引いて現れる演出が行われました。「世界のオザワの演奏は絶対にズレない」という指揮の正確さに目をつけ、演奏開始時間から終了時間を計算、目標到着時間を導き出してブルーインパルスが出発し、演出に成功したと言われています。
青木紘二／アフロスポーツ

in a rugby game. Because of this, he gave up his dream and started conducting music. When he was 24, he moved to Europe to learn more about Western classical music. Soon after he moved, he won a major conducting competition. Some of the world's best conductors saw his talent at this competition.

Ozawa was successful in competitions, but he was not confident. He had trouble finding work and did not have enough money. When the writer Yasushi Inoue visited Paris, he met Ozawa. Ozawa said that he wanted to give up studying in Europe and return to Japan. Inoue told him to keep trying. He said that novels can only reach the world if they are translated into other languages. However, music can be enjoyed by people in any country without translation.

Ozawa was encouraged by Inoue's words, and he decided to keep trying. The famous conductor and composer Leonard Bernstein was very impressed with his work. He let Ozawa become assistant conductor of the New York Philharmonic in 1961. After this, Ozawa became a superstar in the classical music world. He worked as the music director of the Boston Symphony Orchestra for almost 30 years. In 2002, he became the first Asian music director of the Vienna State Opera. Through his life and work, Ozawa showed that music has no borders. ■

■ ケネディ・センター名誉賞授賞式での小澤征爾氏とバラク・オバマ元アメリカ大統領 (2015年12月6日)

この賞は、芸術分野で米国の文化に大きな功績を残した人に贈られます。小澤氏は日本人として初の受賞者となりました。
AP/AFLO

WANT TO LEARN MORE?

Website 小澤征爾公式HP (UNIVERSAL MUSIC) - https://www.universal-music.co.jp/seiji-ozawa/

Book 村上 春樹・小澤 征爾著『小澤征爾さんと、音楽について話をする』新潮社

VOICE DL

Fear or Joy?

Joy of Missing Out

If you feel FOMO,
maybe you need JOMO

■ Google のカンファレンス I/O 2018 でのサンダー・ピチャイ氏

このカンファレンスで行われたサンダー・ピチャイ氏の基調講演では、後ろのスクリーンに「Joy of Missing Out」の文字が映し出されていました。

REUTERS/AFLO

Points for Reading

· FOMO はどのような感情で、どのようなときに起こると説明されていますか。

Digital tools such as the internet and social media have made our lives convenient in many ways. We can now get all kinds of information very easily and communicate with people at any time. Graph 1 shows the percentage of Japanese people (age 6 and over) who have used the internet in the past year. The number was about 100 million in 2022, and this was about 10 times the

05

10

NOTES

00. fear [fíər] 恐れ	28. hunting and gathering 狩猟採集	42. offline [áfláin] オフライン上の、ネットワークに接続されていない
01. digital [dídʒitl] デジタルの	40. CEO 最高経営責任者 (Chief Executive Officer の略)	43. Apple アップル社
02. social media ソーシャルメディア、SNS	40. Google グーグル社	
21. insurance [inʃúərəns] 保険	42. online [ánláin] オンライン上の	
22. Massmutual マスミューチュアル社		

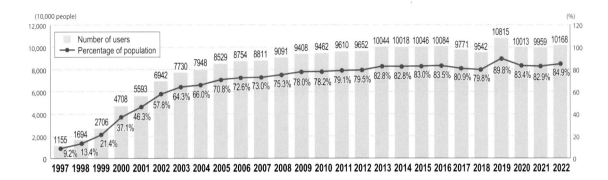

出典：総務省「通信利用動向調査」（2023 年 5 月発表）

number in 1997.

Information from the internet, especially from social media, may give us all kinds of feelings. You may be sad or worried about missing something fun or interesting. This is called FOMO, or "fear of missing out". For example, you could feel FOMO if you saw pictures of your friends at a party or event that you didn't go to. According to a survey by American insurance company Massmutual, more than half of Americans have experienced FOMO at some time.

Why do people feel FOMO? We do not know for sure. One possible reason is from early human history, or the days of hunting and gathering. At that time, people lived in groups and supported each other. Therefore, if you were not a part of the group, your life was in danger. For those people, FOMO was necessary for living.

One way to solve FOMO is called JOMO, or "joy of missing out". This means to get away from digital tools and enjoy the real world around you. Famous technology companies are aware of this. Sundar Pichai, the CEO of Google, talked about JOMO in presentations. He said that people should balance their online and offline lives. Apple also put a "Do Not Disturb" mode on its iPhones. With this mode, you will not be disturbed by phone calls or messages from your phone. Information is important, but we also need balance in our lives. ■

Protecting the City of Water

Venice avoids becoming a "World Heritage in Danger" site – for now

Points for Reading

・「世界危機遺産」とはどのようなもののことですか。
・2023 年 9 月のユネスコの発表はどのようなもので、その理由は何ですか。

■ ベネチア

ベネチアはイタリア北部のアドリア海にある潟湖（海の一部が外海と切り離されてできた浅い湖）にあり、100 を超える島々から構成されています。島の間を約 150 の運河がめぐり、400 以上の橋が街を結んでいます。主な交通手段は船と徒歩であることから「水の都」とも称されます。 Adobestock

NOTES

00. Venice [vénɪs] ベネチア
00. heritage [hérətidʒ] 遺産
05. natural disaster 自然災害
07. UNESCO 国際連合教育科学文化機関（United Nations Educational, Scientific and Cultural Organization）

15. romantic [roumǽntik] ロマンチックな
16. canal [kənǽl] 運河
21. overtourism オーバーツーリズム（観光地が耐えられる以上の観光客が押し寄せる状態）

22. tide [táid] 潮（の干満）
42. moveable [movable] [mú:vəbl] 可動の
45. sea floor 海底

■ MOSE

MOSE の名前は、旧約聖書で水を分断して海を渡ったモーセにちなんで名付けられました。最大で 300cm の高潮を防ぐことができます。 AFP/AFLO

UNESCO World Heritage Sites are places with special history and value. Most of the time, these sites are protected with great care. However, sometimes sites are damaged by war, natural disasters, development, or pollution. In these cases, UNESCO calls them "World Heritage in Danger". Once a site is placed on the "Danger" list, countries are asked to help it. If the site cannot be protected with this help, it may be removed from the World Heritage list.

The city of Venice in Italy has been a World Heritage Site since 1987. People all over the world have a romantic image of its streets and canals. However, that image is in danger. In July 2023, members of UNESCO recommended that Venice should be placed on the "World Heritage in Danger" list. The members' reasons were problems from overtourism and high tides from climate change.

Overtourism is Venice's biggest problem. Too many tourists visit the city every year. This makes the water dirty and makes life difficult for local people. There are now more beds for tourists (49,693) than for local people (49,304).

This is because local people are leaving but more tourists are visiting. High tides have also become a big problem in recent years. When the tide is over 110 centimeters, much of the town is under water. About 100 years ago, tides rose above 110 centimeters only about once a year, but in 2019, this happened 26 times.

The city is taking steps to solve these problems. To reduce the number of tourists, it has started collecting 5 euros from visitors on busy days. To control water levels, it has built a system of moveable gates called MOSE. These gates rise during high tides to prevent water from coming in. When they are not being used, they are put on the sea floor. UNESCO looked at these steps and decided not to put Venice on its "Danger" list in September 2023. However, they said that Venice must take more steps to protect its environment. UNESCO and people all over the world hope that Venice will improve its situation. ■

WANT TO LEARN MORE?

Website UNESCO (英語) - https://www.unesco.org/ja
Website MOSE (英語) - https://www.mosevenezia.eu/?lang=en
Book   宮下 規久朗著『ヴェネツィア ― 美の都の一千年』岩波新書

VOICE DL

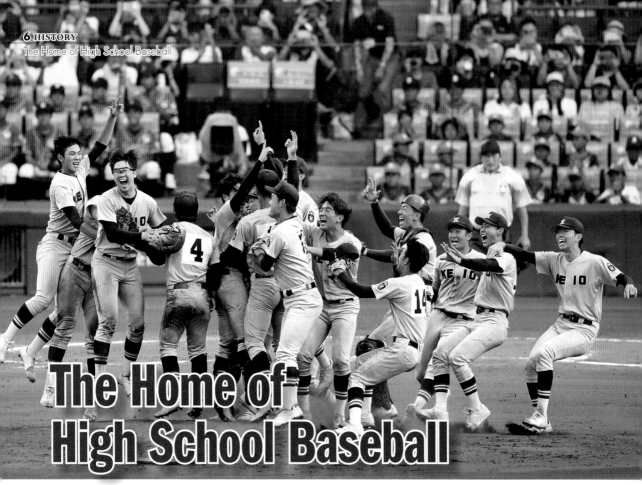

The Home of High School Baseball
Koshien Stadium celebrates 100 years

Points for Reading

・鳴尾球場で開催された高校野球選手権大会は、どのようにして開催されましたか。

■ 第105回全国高等学校野球選手権大会　優勝した慶応義塾高等学校

慶応義塾高等学校は決勝戦で仙台育英学園高等学校を8-2で破り、1916年以来107年ぶりに優勝しました。彼らの部訓「エンジョイ・ベースボール」は大きな話題となりました。

日刊スポーツ/AFLO

In 2024, Koshien Stadium became 100 years old. The stadium was built for the National High School Baseball Championship. High school baseball players all over Japan dream of playing in this stadium.

The National High School Baseball Championship celebrated its 100th year in 2015. This means that the tournament was held before Koshien Stadium was

NOTES

00. home [hóum] 本拠地、本部
03. the National High School Baseball Championship
　　全国高等学校野球選手権大会
05. dream of ～　～を夢見る

19. racecourse [réiskɔ̀ːrs]
　　競走路、競馬場
24. ballpark [bɔ́ːlpɑ̀ːrk]
　　球場、スタジアム
27. flood [flʌd] 洪水

28. control [kəntróul] 制御
31. the Polo Grounds
　　ポロ・グラウンズ
43. major earthquake 大地震

■ 豊中運動場で開催された第1回全国中等学校優勝野球大会（1915年8月）
グラウンドの外野にはフェンスがなかったため、ロープを張ってそれを境界とし、
ノーバウンドで超えた打球が本塁打と見なされました。
毎日新聞社/AFLO

built. The first tournament was held on a ground in Toyonaka, Osaka. Ten schools participated in the tournament. Baseball was already very popular at the time, so many people came to watch it. However, the ground was too small to hold them all. In its third year, the tournament was held at Naruo Stadium in Hyogo. This stadium had a racecourse for horses. Two baseball fields were built inside the racecourse. This way, two games could be played at the same time. However, more and more people came to each tournament, so an even larger ballpark was needed.

At the time, the Muko River near the stadium was being developed for flood control. A new ballpark was built on the land near two rivers that were no longer being used after the development. It was based on the Polo Grounds stadium in New York. The work began in 1924 and

finished quickly. The stadium opened on August 1 of that year. It was large enough to hold 50,000 people. The stadium was named Koshien Stadium. The tenth tournament was held that year, and the tournament also became known as Koshien.

During its long history, the tournament was sometimes cancelled because of war or disease. However, games were held even after major earthquakes. Part of the stadium was damaged by the Great Hanshin-Awaji Earthquake of 1995, but the tournament was still held. In those difficult times, many people were encouraged by the players. The stadium has become loved by baseball fans all over Japan. ■

■ 甲子園球場での花巻東・大谷翔平選手と大阪桐蔭・藤浪晋太郎選手（2012年3月21日）
大谷翔平選手は MLB 移籍後のインタビューで、「僕は甲子園で1回も勝ったことがなかったので、勝ってみたかったというのは今でも思いますね」と語っています。
東京スポーツ/AFLO

WANT TO LEARN MORE?

Website	阪神甲子園球場 - https://www.hanshin.co.jp/koshien/
Website	公益財団法人日本高等学校野球連盟 - https://www.jhbf.or.jp/
Book	玉置 通夫著『甲子園球場物語』文春新書

VOICE DL

Getting Around

Ridesharing is popular worldwide. Will it come to Japan?

■ ライドシェア事業への法規制を求めるデモの様子

2010 年代半ば以降、ライドシェア利用者の安全を確保する規制の必要性が各国で大きな問題となりました。現在は主に 2 つの制度によって規制されています。1 つは米国やアジアで広く採用されている TNC 型ライドシェア法で、規制当局がライドシェア事業者を認可し、事業者が運転手の管理や運行管理を行うものです。もう1 つは欧州などで採用されている PHV 型で、ライドシェア運転手個人が直接認可を受けるものです。

Points for Reading

・日本にライドシェアサービスを導入すべきと考えている人もいますが、その理由は何ですか。

Ridesharing is a service that matches people who need a ride in a car with drivers who can pick them up. It can be used easily with a smartphone app. The user chooses a place to go with the
05
app. After a short time, the user gets information about available drivers near them. Once the user selects a driver, the car will come and pick them up in a few minutes. Ridesharing services
10

NOTES

00. get around 　あちこち移動する、動き回る	06. app [ǽp] 　アプリ (application の短縮語)	38. crime [kráim] 犯罪 (行為)
00. ridesharing ライドシェア	08. select [səlékt] 選択する	
03. pick 〜 up 〜を車に乗せる、車で 　迎えに行く	17. license [láisəns] 許可証、免許証	
	27. rural [rúərəl] 田舎の、地方の	
	28. aging [éidʒiŋ] 高齢化の進む	

■ ライドシェアアプリ「Grab」の使用画面

ライドシェアサービスは、2009年に米国カリフォルニア州で創業したUber Technologies社が主導し、米国や欧州、アジアで急速に拡大しました。他に、米国のLyft社やシンガポールのGrab社などのサービスがあります。

are widely used around the world. However, the Japanese government has not yet fully allowed them.

There are several differences between rytesharing and Japanese taxis. One is that unlike taxi drivers, ridesharing drivers do not need a special license. Another is that the car used for ridesharing does not have to be a special car like a taxi. In other words, anyone with a driver's license and a car can become a ridesharing driver.

Some people say that ridesharing services should be allowed in Japan. The biggest reason for this is the decrease in the number of buses and taxis. This is especially true in rural areas with aging populations. In such areas, there are many elderly people who cannot drive cars. Ridesharing is likely to be useful in those areas. And most of all, ridesharing services are often cheaper and more convenient than taxis.

Taxi companies in Japan are asking the government not to allow full ridesharing services. The companies say that accidents and crimes will increase because ridesharing drivers do not have special licenses. And they are worried that fewer people will use taxis. In 2024, the government allowed taxi companies to provide ridesharing services in some areas. They only provide ridesharing services when there are not enough taxis. The government says it will take time to decide whether to allow full ridesharing. ■

■ 超党派ライドシェア勉強会の小泉進次郎会長から提言書を受け取る岸田文雄首相

小泉氏は日本版ライドシェアの全国での導入を早急に進めることなどを求める提言書を首相に提出し、全面解禁に向けた法整備について、「年内に結論を出していただきたい」と求めました。

毎日新聞社/AFLO

Hemingway is 125

The Nobel Prize winner put his life into his books

Points for Reading

・ヘミングウェイの生涯はどのようなものでしたか。

・ヘミングウェイの小説の特徴は何ですか。

■『誰がために鐘は鳴る』執筆中のヘミングウェイ（1939 年撮影）

ヘミングウェイは毎朝 6 時頃から正午くらいまで執筆をしたあと、毎日どこまで書き進めたかを大きな表に記していたという記録が残っています。また、椅子を使わず立ったまま執筆することも多かったと言われています。

Ernest Hemingway is known as one of the greatest American writers of the 20th century. However, his life was as interesting as his books. In fact, many of his books are based on his experiences. His first novel, *The Sun Also Rises*, was based on his time in Paris. *A Farewell to Arms* was based on his experience as an 05

NOTES

00. Nobel Prize winner ノーベル賞受賞者	09. ambulance [ǽmbjələns] 救急車	28. the Spanish Civil War スペイン内戦
06. *The Sun Also Rises* 『日はまた昇る』	09. *The Old Man and the Sea* 『老人と海』	32. plane crash 飛行機墜落事故
07. *A Farewell to Arms* 『武器よさらば』	13. literature [lítərətʃər] 文学	41. memory loss 記憶喪失［障害］
	21. iceberg [áisbəːrg] 氷山	42. shotgun [ʃátgʌn] 散弾銃
	21. theory [θíːəri] 理論	

■ 運転手として勤務中のヘミングウェイ（1918 年撮影）

19 歳のときには自ら志願してアメリカ赤十字の救急車の運転手になりました。北イタリアのフォッサルタ戦線での負傷者搬送中に、砲撃を受け負傷しました。

GRANGER.COM/AFLO

■ ライオンを仕留めたヘミングウェイ（1934 年撮影、ケニア）

ヘミングウェイは幼少期に父親に狩猟を教わりました。ヘミングウェイの死因は当初散弾銃の暴発によるものとされていましたが、彼が銃の扱いに慣れていたことや遺書の発見により自殺と断定されました。

TopFoto/AFLO

ambulance driver in World War I. *The Old Man and the Sea* was inspired by his love of fishing and the outdoors. For that book, he won the 1954 Nobel Prize in Literature.

Hemingway became famous for his unique style of writing. When he was 17, he began working as a newspaper writer. As a reporter, he was taught to write short and powerful sentences, and he also used this style when he started writing novels. His writing is based on his "iceberg" theory. This means that only a small part of the story can be seen, like an iceberg in the ocean. The rest of the story is imagined by the reader.

Hemingway was known as a very active man who loved adventure. He was injured in World War I, but he went to the Spanish Civil War and World War II to work as a reporter. He loved hunting wild animals and often traveled to Cuba and Africa. During a trip to Africa in 1954, he was in two plane crashes, but he survived. In addition to these adventures, he was known for his love of fighting and drinking.

Because of his lifestyle and his novels, Hemingway became the image of a "strong man" in the 20th century. However, his life became much harder in his later years. His accidents in Africa gave him a lot of pain and memory loss. He ended his life with a shotgun in 1961. Since Hemingway's time, the image of a "strong man" has changed. However, he will always be remembered for his powerful life and work. ■

WANT TO LEARN MORE?

Book	アーネスト・ヘミングウェイ著『日はまた昇る』新潮文庫
Book	アーネスト・ヘミングウェイ著『武器よさらば』新潮文庫
Book	アーネスト・ヘミングウェイ著『老人と海』新潮文庫

VOICE DL

Medicines on Wheels

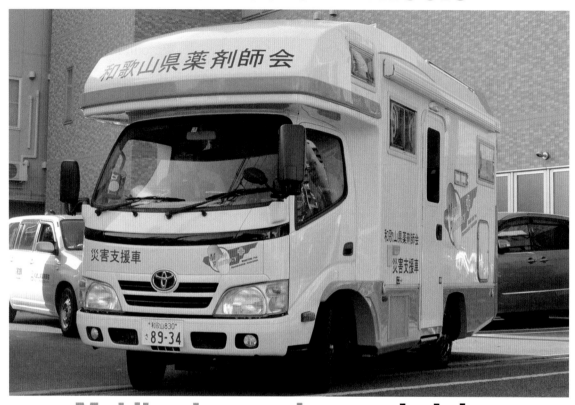

Mobile pharmacies are helping in disaster areas

Points for Reading

・東日本大震災ではどのような問題が起きましたか。
・薬局が少ない地方では、薬はどのように供給されていますか。

■ 和歌山県から能登半島に向かうモバイルファーマシー

災害発生後、重症患者の救命措置のため48時間以内にDMAT（災害派遣医療チーム）が派遣されます。DMAT撤退後は、長期的な医療支援のためにJMAT（日本医師会災害医療チーム）が活動します。いずれのチームにも薬剤師が所属しており、モバイルファーマシーを拠点に医薬品の供給や避難所の衛生管理を行います。
朝日新聞

On January 1, 2024, a major earthquake occurred in Japan. Areas in Ishikawa Prefecture received heavy damage. Many houses fell down, and aftershocks continued. To avoid danger, people had to live in evacuation shelters.

05

NOTES

00. mobile [móubl] 移動式の、可動性の	06. evacuation shelter （災害時の）避難所	29. the Miyagi Prefecture Pharmaceutical Association 宮城県薬剤師会
00. pharmacy [fáːrməsi] 薬局	21. the 2011 Great East Japan Earthquake 2011年東日本大震災	31. camper [kǽmpər] キャンピングカー
02. occur [əkɔ́ːr] 発生する、起こる	27. pharmacist [fáːrməsist] 薬剤師	43. rural [rúərəl] 地方の、田舎の
05. aftershock [ǽftərʃɑ̀k] 余震		

■ モバイルファーマシー内の様子
車内には冷蔵保存が必要な医薬品の管理や、無菌状態で調剤できる設備が
あります。

朝日新聞

People in shelters need medicines for many reasons. First, many people take medicines regularly. They may run out of their medicines if they have to stay in a shelter for a long time. Also, diseases spread easily when large groups of people are sharing the same place. Living in a shelter is hard, so people feel better if they know that they can get the medicines they need.

One way to help people in shelters after disasters is to send mobile pharmacy vehicles. The mobile pharmacy idea is based on lessons from the 2011 Great East Japan Earthquake. Hospitals and pharmacies were damaged in that disaster, and the areas did not have enough medicines. Even when medicines arrived, it was difficult to deliver them to people because pharmacists were needed to prepare the medicines. To solve this problem, the Miyagi Prefecture Pharmaceutical Association developed a mobile pharmacy using a camper. The camper has electric power and can hold equipment for preparing medicines. It also has a bed and toilet, so pharmacists can stay at disaster sites for many hours or days. The Miyagi association introduced the idea to other prefectures. The vehicles were helpful after the earthquakes in Kumamoto in 2016 and in Ishikawa in 2024.

Mobile pharmacies could be useful not only for disaster areas, but also for rural areas with few or no pharmacies. In some of these areas, doctors give medicines directly to patients. If mobile pharmacies could visit these areas regularly, the pharmacists could give medicines to patients. This would allow doctors to give more time to their patients. Mobile pharmacies may become part of people's lives in various ways. ■

WANT TO LEARN MORE?

Website 日本薬剤師会 - https://www.nichiyaku.or.jp/
Website 厚生労働省 DMAT 事務局 - http://www.dmat.jp/
Book 井手口 直子著『薬剤師になるには』ぺりかん社

VOICE DL

Are EVs Really Clean?
They may release more CO$_2$ over their lifecycles

Points for Reading

・電気自動車とガソリン車のどちらが環境によいかを考えるとき、どのようなことを検討する必要がありますか。

■ 充電中の電気自動車

2023 年 4 月時点で、フル充電の状態で最も長い距離の走行が可能な電気自動車は、米国ルシード・モータース社の「ルシード・エア」です。その距離は約 830kmで、東京都から広島県まで走行できることになります。

椿雅人 /AFLO

One of the keys to stopping global warming is switching to electric vehicles (EVs) from gasoline-powered vehicles. Electric cars, buses, and trucks can be found in cities all over the world. EVs do not release CO$_2$ into the air

05

NOTES

01. global warming 地球温暖化
02. electric vehicle 電気自動車
03. gasoline-powered ガソリン駆動の
13. the International Energy Agency 国際エネルギー機関
17. lithium-ion リチウムイオン
17. battery [bǽtəri] バッテリー、電池
19. rare metal レアメタル、希少金属
28. renewable energy 再生可能エネルギー
29. charge [tʃɑːrdʒ] 〜に充電する
31. fossil fuel 化石燃料
39. per 〜 〜当たり、〜ごとに
50. impact on 〜 〜に対する影響

when they are used. But are they really cleaner than gasoline-powered vehicles?

To find out, we have to look at a vehicle's lifecycle, from making it to throwing it away. For EVs, the "making" part uses the most energy. According to the International Energy Agency, making an EV produces twice as much CO_2 as making a gasoline-powered vehicle. This is because lithium-ion batteries, the most important part of an EV, require lots of energy to make. They also require rare metals, and getting these rare metals uses a lot of energy. At the "making" stage, gasoline-powered vehicles are often cleaner than EVs.

If you buy an EV, when does it become cleaner than a gasoline-powered vehicle? This depends on many things. For example, what kind of vehicle is it, and where is it used? Also, is renewable energy used to charge the battery? If the energy comes from coal or other fossil fuels, it will produce CO_2. One study found that EVs in the EU become cleaner after about 77,000 kilometers. In Japan, however, EVs become cleaner

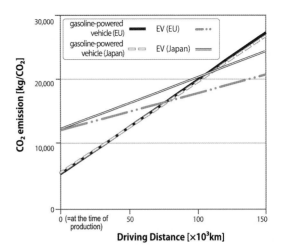

■ ガソリン車と EV のライフサイクルにおける CO_2 排出量

出典：Estimation of CO_2 Emissions of Internal Combustion Engine Vehicle and Battery Electric Vehicle Using LCA

after about 110,000 kilometers. That is because less renewable energy is used in Japan. People drive their cars in Japan an average of about 6,000 kilometers per year. Therefore, it may take around 18 years for an EV to become cleaner. This is much longer than most people in Japan use a car.

More attention is being given to vehicle lifecycles. This includes how energy is produced and how the vehicle and its battery can be recycled. The EU is asking companies to share this information, and Japan will soon do the same. When we think about EVs, we will need to consider their total impact on the environment. ■

WANT TO LEARN MORE?

Website　ゼロカーボンドライブ（環境省 HP）- https://www.env.go.jp/air/zero_carbon_drive/
Book　　加藤 康子他著『EV（電気自動車）推進の罠「脱炭素」政策の嘘』　ワニブックス
Book　　川辺 謙一著『図解まるわかり 電気自動車のしくみ』　翔泳社

VOICE DL

Cleaning Up Space

Astroscale is taking on a problem that was thought to be impossible

Points for Reading

・スペースデブリについてどのような問題がありますか。
・アストロスケール社はどのような企業ですか。

■ スペースデブリ（宇宙ごみ）
これまでに宇宙ごみが衝突したことが原因と確認されている、人工衛星が破壊された事例は3例あります。いずれも衛星が大破、または通信が途絶えています。

NASA/Science Photo Library/AFLO

Without satellites, our lives would be very different. We rely on them for many things, from internet and GPS to weather forecasting and national security. In December 2023, about 9,000 active satellites were going around the Earth. There may be over 100,000 in the next few years. These satellites are very helpful when they are working well. However, if they break or crash into something while in space, they cause problems.

"Space debris" is the name for pieces of trash in space. Debris can be from broken satellites, spacecraft and rockets, and even toothbrushes and gloves used by astronauts. There are 23,000 pieces of debris larger than 10 cm, and about 100 million pieces larger than 1 mm. They move at 24,000 km/h, and they

NOTES

01. satellite [sǽtəlàit] 人工衛星	13. debris [dəbríː] 残骸、破片	39. aim to *do* ～することを目指す
03. GPS 全地球測位システム (global positioning system)	15. spacecraft [spéiskræft] 宇宙機、宇宙船	39. launch [lɔ́ːntʃ] 打ち上げる
04. weather forecasting 天気 [気象] 予報	17. astronaut [ǽstrənɔ̀ːt] 宇宙飛行士	43. atmosphere [ǽtməsfìər] 大気 (圏)
04. national security 国の安全 (保障)	27. startup company スタートアップ企業	

can destroy active satellites and other spacecraft. There are no international rules about cleaning up space debris, so many companies just leave it there. Controlling this problem is a very important issue for space research.

A Japanese startup company called Astroscale is working to solve this issue. It was started by Nobu Okada. He used to work for the Japanese government. He thought that cleaning up space debris could become a new business. However, space debris is very difficult to catch because it moves very quickly. People told Okada that the problem may be impossible to solve. "If there's no solution, I will find one," he said.

Astroscale aims to launch spacecraft that can safely find and catch pieces of debris. It will approach the fast-moving debris and catch it. Then it will drop the debris into the Earth's atmosphere so that it burns up. Ten years ago, there was no market for cleaning up space debris. However, the market could be two trillion yen in the next 10 years. Thanks to Astroscale, more companies will enter the market and try to solve the space debris problem. ■

■ 宇宙ごみ除去衛星「ELSA-d」の実物大模型と岡田光信氏
ELSA-d は、軌道上での技術実証を行うために 2021 年 3 月 23 日に打ち上げられました。ELSA-d は捕獲衛星と、デブリ化した衛星を模した模擬デブリ衛星から構成されています。同年 8 月には、この模擬デブリ衛星の捕獲に成功しました。こうした技術が評価され、2023 年 9 月、アストロスケール社はアメリカ宇宙軍から衛星の燃料補給技術の開発を 2,550 万ドルで受注しました。
つのだよしお/AFLO

WANT TO LEARN MORE?
Website アストロスケール（英語）- https://astroscale.com/
Website JAXA スペースデブリ対策 - https://www.jaxa.jp/projects/debris/
Book 八坂 哲雄著『宇宙のゴミ問題 − スペース・デブリ』 裳華房

VOICE DL

NEWSBREAKS
for BASIC English Learners
2024

ニュースブレイク 2024 年　ベーシック
定価 600 円＋税
付録【設問集・解答解説書・課題テスト】

初版発行：2024 年　6 月　3 日
2 版発行：2024 年　6 月 17 日

本 書 著 者　Kevin Glenz・小林義昌
編 集 協 力　田澤 仁
発 行 所　株式会社 エミル出版

本社　〒102-0072　東京都千代田区飯田橋 2-8-1
　　　【電　　　話】03-6272-5481
　　　【ファックス】03-6272-5482

本書の「解答解説書（付録）」および「課題テスト（付録）」は、先生からのお申し出をいただいたときに限り、お届け致します。

■ 写真・資料図版提供（順不同、敬称略）
AFLO、gettyimages ほか

■ CD ナレーション
Kevin Glenz ほか

■ 表紙写真
ベネチア　大運河
Adobe Stock

© 2024 EMILE PUBLISHING
ISBN978-4-86449-182-2